Your Choice, Snoopy

Charles M. Schulz

CORONET BOOKS
Hodder Fawcett Ltd., London

Copyright © 1967 by United
Feature Syndicate Inc.
First published by Fawcett Publications Inc.,
New York 1973
Coronet edition 1974
Second impression 1975

This book comprises the first half of *You're
Something Else, Charlie Brown*, and is reprinted by
arrangement with Holt, Rinehart & Winston, Inc.

This book is sold subject to the condition that
it shall not, by way of trade or otherwise, be
lent, re-sold, hired out or otherwise circulated
without the publisher's prior consent in any
form of binding or cover other than that in
which this is published and without a similar
condition including this condition being
imposed on the subsequent purchaser.

Printed and bound in Great Britain for
Coronet Books,
Hodder Fawcett Ltd,
St. Paul's House, Warwick Lane,
London, EC4P 4AH
by Hazell Watson & Viney Ltd,
Aylesbury, Bucks

ISBN 0 340 18663 1

BIRDS THINK I HAVE A NICE FACE!

➤

CLOMP!

I KNOW A SPIT-BALL IS ILLEGAL, BUT I WONDER ABOUT A DROOL-BALL?

BONK!

I'LL NEVER BE A GOOD MANAGER....
I HATE TO AWAKEN AN INFIELDER
WHO'S SLEEPING SO PEACEFULLY!

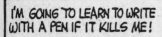

DEAR PEN PAL,
TODAY I TAKE PEN
IN HAND.

I AM VERY PROUD
OF MYSELF.

SO FAR I HAVEN'T
SMEARED A SINGLE

WOO

PAT
PAT
PAT
PAT

THEY COME DEPRESSED, AND THEY GO AWAY FEELING GREAT

MY BROTHER PATS BIRDS ON THE HEAD

WHAT?

THAT'S THE USUAL REACTION

SORRY, BIRD..

SCHULZ

BOOT!

"THIS IS 'BE KIND TO ANIMALS WEEK'"

WELL, SNOOPY, HERE WE ARE AT SUMMER CAMP...

THE FIRST THING THEY'LL DO IS ASSIGN US TO A BARRACKS, AND THEN WE'LL HAVE LUNCH...

NOT "LUNCH"... CHOW! WE WORLD WAR I FLYING ACES ALWAYS CALL IT "CHOW"...WHAT A MISERABLE CAMP.. WE MUST BE FIFTY KILOMETERS FROM THE NEAREST VILLAGE! CURSE THIS HOT WEATHER! CURSE THIS STUPID WAR!

WE WORLD WAR I FLYING ACES DO A LOT OF GRIPING!

SCHULZ

➤

RIGHT IN THE MIDDLE OF A BALL GAME?

ARE YOU OUT OF YOUR MIND?!!

I'M TRYING TO PITCH, CAN'T YOU SEE THAT?!!! I'VE GOT TO CONCENTRATE ON WHAT I'M DOING!

OH, NOW YOU'RE GOING TO BE HURT, AREN'T YOU? OH, GOOD GRIEF, ALL RIGHT... COME HERE...

SKRITCH
SKRITCH
SKRITCH
SKRITCH
SKRITCH

SIGH!

NO WONDER SANDY KOUFAX RETIRED!

➤

CHUCK, I'D LIKE TO HAVE YOU MEET JOSÉ PETERSON..

NOW, THE WAY I SEE IT, CHUCK, YOU CAN PLAY JOSÉ PETERSON HERE AT SECOND WHERE HE CAN WORK WITH THAT FUNNY-LOOKING KID YOU'VE GOT PLAYING SHORTSTOP...

WHAT ABOUT LINUS? HE'S ALWAYS PLAYED A PRETTY GOOD SECOND BASE...

DON'T WORRY ABOUT LINUS... I'LL EXPLAIN THE WHOLE THING TO HIM..

HI, SWEETIE!

THAT'S THE WAY JOSÉ PETERSON HIT THE YEAR HIS FAMILY LIVED IN NEW MEXICO...

THAT'S THE WAY JOSÉ PETERSON HIT THE YEAR HIS FAMILY LIVED IN NORTH DAKOTA...

NOW, LOOK, CHUCK... HERE'S THE WAY YOUR NEW LINEUP CAN GO...

WITH JOSÉ PETERSON AT SECOND AND ME TAKING OVER THE MOUND CHORES, YOU'RE GOING TO HAVE A GREAT TEAM, YES, SIR!

NOBODY WILL BE ABLE TO BEAT US! WHY, YOU'LL PROBABLY BE SELECTED "MANAGER OF THE YEAR"!

FOR WHAT?

YOUR BROTHER PATS BIRDS ON THE HEAD!

THAT'S A **TERRIBLE** THING TO SAY TO SOMEONE THE FIRST THING IN THE MORNING!

NOW, I'VE SEEN EVERYTHING...

A BIRD HIPPIE!

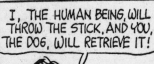

I DON'T UNDERSTAND YOU...
WHY DO YOU HAVE TO PLAY
SHORTSTOP WITH YOUR
SUPPER DISH IN YOUR MOUTH?

BECAUSE I DON'T HAVE
A POCKET!

CHARLIE BROWN?
CHARLIE BROWN?
ARE YOU IN HERE?
IT'S ME..LINUS...
ARE YOU IN HERE?

YES, I'M IN HERE! GO AWAY! I DON'T WANT TO SEE ANYONE! AND DON'T PULL UP THAT SHADE!

I JUST WANT TO LIE HERE IN THE DARK, AND FORGET ABOUT EVERYTHING!

BUT WHAT ABOUT THE BALL TEAM?

ESPECIALLY THE STUPID BALL TEAM!

I SUPPOSE I COULD LIE HERE IN THE DARK FOR THE REST OF MY LIFE...

IT'S KIND OF NICE TO BE ABLE TO WITHDRAW FROM ALL YOUR PROBLEMS. IT'S NICE TO BE ABLE TO FORGET YOUR RESPONSIBILITIES, AND....

RESPONSIBILITIES?!! GOOD GRIEF, I FORGOT TO FEED MY DOG!

VERY PECULIAR LOOKING WAITER...PROBABLY SOME POOR BLIGHTER JUST OUT OF THE TRENCHES!

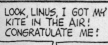

HERE ARE THE LATEST
CORONET PEANUTS TITLES

*All these books are available at your bookshop or newsagent, or
can be ordered direct from the publisher. Just tick the titles you
want and fill in the form below.*

CORONET BOOKS, P.O. Box 11, Falmouth, Cornwall.

Please send cheque or postal order. No currency, and allow the
following for postage and packing:

1 book – 10p, 2 books – 15p, 3 books – 20p, 4–5 books – 25p, 6–9
books – 4p per copy, 10–15 books – 2½p per copy, 16–30 books 2p
per copy, over 30 books free within the U.K.

Overseas – please allow 10p for the first book and 5p per copy for
each additional book.

Name ....

Address ....

....